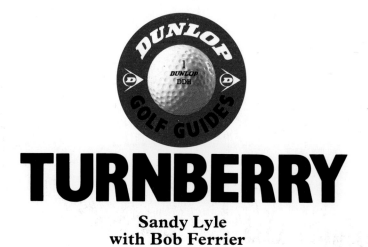

TURNBERRY

Sandy Lyle
with Bob Ferrier

World's Work Ltd

First published 1982 by
World's Work Ltd
The Windmill Press
Kingswood, Tadworth, Surrey

Paintings by Ken Turner
Photography by David Pocknell

Copyright © Lennard Books Ltd 1982

SBN 437 09063 9

Made by Lennard Books
The Old School
Wheathampstead, Herts AL4 8AN

Editor Michael Leitch
Designed by David Pocknell's Company Ltd
Production Reynolds Clark Associates Ltd
Printed and bound in Belgium by
Henri Proost & Cie, Turnhout

Back cover photograph by
Lawrence Levy

TURNBERRY

Of all the great Scottish links, the Ailsa Course at the Turnberry Hotel is the most dramatic, the most spectacular and the most compellingly beautiful. Set along a rock-bound coast, above the golden sweep of the sands of Turnberry Bay, the Ailsa is a fine championship course made doubly magnificent by the surrounding landscape. Across the water to the north-west stands the great bulk of the Island of Arran with its towering peaks; beyond it to the west lies the long, low peninsula of Kintyre; to the south-west is the massive granite outcrop of Ailsa Craig, marking the southern end of the famed Firth of Clyde; and to the east are the rich, ripe, rolling farmlands of Carrick. All of this makes the Ailsa a marvellous place of blinding sunsets and sea mists and long Scottish gloamings, and, it should be said, from time to time – storms.

There are two Turnberry courses. The Arran, slightly less testing, flatter and running through avenues of gorse, lies 'inside' the Ailsa. Jointly they have had an uneven history. Originally the third Marquis of Ailsa commissioned Willie Fernie to design 13 holes, for the use no doubt of his local tenants. Willie Fernie was professional at Troon from 1887–1924, and his son Tom became the first professional at Turnberry. The third Marquis combined landowning with being a director of the Glasgow & South-Western Railway Company and, in 1899, captain of Prestwick Golf Club. At the turn of the century he leased land at Turnberry to the railway company. By 1905, Fernie had designed and laid out a second course of 13 holes, and the hotel had been completed as possibly the first hotel/golf complex in the world.

With the amalgamation of the railway companies into four main groups in 1926, Turnberry became the property of the London, Midland & Scottish Railway Company, and before British Railways chairman Dr Beeching came along in the 1960s with his celebrated 'axe', it was possible to board a sleeping car at London's Euston Station and emerge next morning in the hotel, virtually untouched by the weather.

The courses scarcely had time to settle before World War I, when the Royal Flying Corps used the ground as a pilot training station, with much resultant damage. After the war, the newer 'number two' course became the major course, and was named after the third Marquis. Between the wars an experienced architect, Major C. K. Hutchison, who had worked on the newer Gleneagles Hotel courses, was engaged to lengthen the Ailsa and eliminate some blind shots, changes which had been completed by 1938. World War II was a disaster for golf at Turnberry. RAF Coastal Command constructed an air base on the courses – many thought unnecessarily! – and littered the area with enormous buildings and concrete runways, some of them 18in thick. So convulsed was the ground that many Whitehall mandarins, and indeed some of the hotel company's directors, were convinced that Turnberry was finished as a golfing centre. However, Frank Hole, managing director of British Transport Hotels Ltd, by then the owners, thought otherwise. After a bitter and perhaps bloody-minded battle, he extracted from the government of the day enough financial compensation to underwrite the entire rebuilding of the courses. Jimmy Alexander, BTH's superintendent of grounds and golf courses, with Suttons of Reading as contractors, re-made golf at Turnberry to the designs of Mackenzie Ross, the golf architect. Between them, they produced a masterpiece: the present Ailsa course.

By June 1951 courses were completed, and over the next two decades the Ailsa was to stage an Amateur Championship, two PGA Match Play Championships, two Scottish Professional Championships, the Home Internationals, a Walker Cup match, and many professionally sponsored tournaments. The final accolade came with its first Open, the 106th Open Championship of 1977, and perhaps the most astonishing of all in modern times. That year Jack Nicklaus and Tom Watson scored three identical rounds of 68, 70, and 66, and were paired in the final round, when Watson scored 65 and Nicklaus 66. In the quality of their stroke-making, and in the valour of their temperaments, Watson and Nicklaus fashioned one of the greatest battles ever known in championship golf. And oddly, although the championship was played in generally fine conditions, only one other player, Hubert Green, was under par for the week.

For the professionals, from the championship tees, the Ailsa Course is difficult. For amateurs, from the medal tees, the Ailsa Course is still difficult! Yet it is not harshly or brutally difficult, and I believe it is essentially fair. The fairways are reasonably generous and provide few awkward stances, and on the whole I make it one of our finest links courses. Your only problem at Turnberry may be that the dramatic beauty of your surroundings will distract you from the work at hand.

Top left: The main entrance
to the Turnberry Hotel
Top right: Evening sun on the
Ailsa Course

Above: Turnberry Hotel from
the course and, left, the
Dormy House, the course and
the lighthouse from the hotel

Turnberry Hotel Golf Courses

AILSA COURSE Local Rules

1 **Out of Bounds**
A ball is out of bounds if it lies:
(a) Beyond any fence bounding the course (as at the 1st, 3rd and 18th holes).
(b) Over the garden wall at the 9th hole.

2 **Water Hazards**
The beach at the 9th hole and the burn at the 7th, 16th and holes are ordinary water hazards. (Rule 33/2 applies).

3 **Lateral Water Hazard**
The beach at the 10th hole is a lateral water hazard. (Rule applies).

4 **Roads and Paths**
(a) The Lighthouse Road crossing the 9th hole and on the right 13th and 14th holes is an obstruction. (Rule 31/2 applies).
(b) A ball lying on or within one club length of the footpath 18th hole may be lifted and dropped without penalty kept point from which the ball was lifted between the player hole, but not nearer the hole.
(c) A ball lying on the gravel surface surrounding the club be lifted and dropped without penalty within two club the gravel, but not nearer the hole.

5 **Obstructions**
The direction stone at the 9th hole is an immovable o (Rule 31/2 applies).

6 **Tarmac Areas**
All tarmac areas within the boundaries of the course are in of the course.
Note:- The ball must be played as it lies or be declared (Rule 29/2).

7 **Pop-up Sprinkler Heads**
All pop-up sprinkler heads are immovable obstruction from interference by them may be obtained under R addition, if such obstruction intervene between the ball the player may obtain relief without penalty in th circumstances :
(a) If the ball lie on the putting green, it may be lifted an nearer the hole, at the nearest point at which such i the obstruction is avoided.
(b) If the ball lie off the putting green (but not in a within two club lengths of the intervening obstruc lifted, cleaned and dropped as in clause (a) above.

Left: The Championship tee at the 9th and, inset, a spectacular view to the south

		CHAMPIONSHIP		MEDAL S.S.S. 71		STROKE INDEX (AND LADIES)					LGU LA
		LENGTH IN YARDS	PAR	LENGTH IN YARDS	PAR						LENGTH IN YARDS
1	Ailsa Craig	362	4	362	4	9					
2	Mak Siccar	428	4	378	4	13					345
3	Blaw Wearie	462	4	393	4	5					367
4	Woe-be-Tide	167	3	167	3	17					381
5	Fin'me oot	477	5	411	4	3					112
6	Tappie Toorie	222	3	222	3	15					393
7	Roon the Ben	528	5	465	4	1					219
8	Goat Fell	427	4	427	4	11					424
9	Bruce's Castle	455	4	413	4	7					385
OUT		3528	36	3238	34						372
10	Dinna Fouter	452	4	430	4	6					2998 3
11	Maidens	177	3	137	3	18					339
12	Monument	391	4	391	4	8					130 3
13	Tickly Tap	411	4	379	4	14					358 4
14	Risk-an-Hope	440	4	400	4	2					338 4
15	Ca Canny	209	3	168	3	16					395 5
16	Wee Burn	409	4	381	4	10					160 3
17	Lang Whang	500	5	487	5	4					343 4
18	Ailsa Hame	431	4	377	4	12					401 5
IN		3420	35	3150	35						374 4
TOTAL		6948	71	6388	69						2838 36
											5836 75

GROSS	HANDICAP	N

Turnberry Hotel Golf Courses

TURNBERRY HOTEL

Practice Ground

Club House

1 ARRAN COURSE

1 AILSA COURSE

AILSA CRAIG

1

362 YDS/331M

PAR 4

STROKE 9

In common with the opening holes at Troon, St Andrews, and possibly even Carnoustie, the Ailsa start is fairly benign, as though to encourage you for the delights, or otherwise, to come. The hole should be a comfortable two-shot par 4, and I suspect its defences look slightly more daunting than they are. It dog-legs to the right at around the 200-yard mark, turning and appearing to narrow between two sets of bunkers set in the rough on either side. There is in fact a cluster of two large and two small bunkers on the right stretching from 210 to 250 yards. On the left are two bunkers which have recently been intentionally grassed over forming no more than awkward mounds at 200 and 220 yards. The rough on the right side can be quite severe and all the bunkers are reachable from the front tees unless you are driving into a particularly strong wind.

The ideal drive should put you in the left half of the fairway, giving you the optimum angle of attack on the green. Thus your line may well be dead-centre between the bunkers and the mounds on the left, if anything favouring the left side. If you are past the mounds and in the fairway, you are ideally placed. The front centre and front right of the green are closed off tightly by a very purposeful bunker. There is another to the back left. A slight dip occurs in front of the green, which is built up but quite flat with no major contours to worry about, either on the approach shot or in putting.

On the right side of the green, behind the front bunker, is a

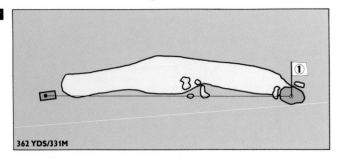

Ailsa Craig is named after the famous Ailsa rock in the Firth of Clyde, visible from almost every part of the course.

Left:
A closer view of the green shows clearly the large front bunker and the downslope to the right of the green

362 YDS/331M

Bunker guarding front centre and front right of the green

Cluster of bunkers at 210–250 yards

2nd shot at the 1st

downslope, so if you miss the green on that side the ball can be thrown right and scuttle down into some bushes. If you decide you cannot carry the front bunker and fly the ball all the way to the putting surface, think of playing to the left of that bunker, taking a line for your second shot on the bunker at the left back. At the left end of the

front bunker, at the left entrance to the green, is an attractive patch of fairway, from which you might plan to chip (and, of course, one-putt home).

You must work hard to make no more than four on this opening hole. On a course like the Ailsa you are bound to drop strokes, so drop them at a hole which has much stiffer defences

than this one. If I started a championship with a five, I would be very disappointed.

If this makes the opening hole sound fairly routine, it remains true that the first half-dozen holes of the Ailsa constitute a difficult beginning, and it is important to get into top gear quickly. Allow time to hit some balls on the practice ground before

you start, and be properly warmed to the task. In the 1979 European Open, I birdied six of the first seven holes to give myself an 8-shot lead, having started the round one shot behind. That broke the back of the round, and won me the championship. The one hole I didn't birdie was the second.

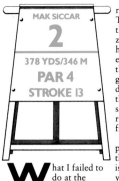

MAK SICCAR

2

378 YDS/346 M

PAR 4

STROKE 13

What I failed to do at the second in 1979 (see previous page) was 'mak siccar', or make sure, since I missed the green badly to the left, but managed to pitch up from the depths of the rough and hole the putt for a par.

The second I find an interesting hole which also has a good deal in common with the third. Neither hole needs a fairway bunker to compromise or direct the drive. At the second, you must drive up to a fairway set along a right-hand ridge. Your line could be slightly to the

right of the distant flag. The immediate rough on the right, in the driving zone, is not all that heavy, but along the entire left side, from there to the green, the ground falls quite sharply down to the parallel third fairway and these slopes have very telling rough. So keep away from the left side.

Having got into position, you find that the architect of the Ailsa is still not finished with you. In your line to the centre of the green is a big fairway bunker, some 60 yards from the front edge of the green and perhaps 80 yards from the flagstick; a secondary, supporting bunker lurks 20 yards behind it. The green is big, possibly 40 yards long. There is a bunker just short of the left front, with downslopes continuing to the left of it. There is a bigger bunker at the right front, with mounds and slopes around it, but there is a reasonably wide entrance to the green so that you can get at it from either

the left or right side of the fairway. But to have any chance at all with this hole, you must be on the fairway with the tee shot.

At best, the second

shot will be long, perhaps as much as 170 yards, and you must carry these two fairway bunkers. They have the effect of foreshortening the hole, and it is

Ground slopes steeply away on the left side of the fairway

If you are likely to be short, be short on the right

Approach to the 2nd green

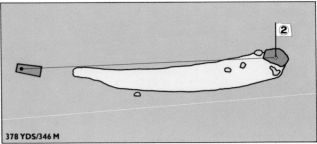

378 YDS/346 M

there are few worries past the pin and plenty of space beyond the central fairway bunkers. If you must be short, be short of the right, greenside bunker; from there you will have a clear and open chip or pitch to the flag. All in all, this hole is quite a testy par 4.

The larger bunker covering the right of the green

difficult to judge exactly how far you have to go. Put your faith in the yardage and hit a positive, optimistic shot with the correct club. Do not be afraid to be up –

What's in the name?

The name of the 2nd hole is its motto too – 'Make sure' with every shot you play.

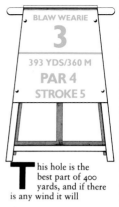

BLAW WEARIE

3

393 YDS/360 M

PAR 4

STROKE 5

This hole is the best part of 400 yards, and if there is any wind it will probably be dead against, so you have to face up to two quite long hits. As you stand on the tee, you will see that the hole takes you down a shallow valley, the fairway turning slightly right, and from the tee you can see virtually nothing of the green at all. The fairway is narrow, the green is narrow, and the third hole vies with the 9th and 14th as the toughest par 4 you will meet on this course.

Like the second, the third hole has no fairway bunkering in play for the drive. The right side of the fairway falls off, down towards the fifth fairway, in a sharp slope scarred with deep gullies covered in strong and dangerous rough. The left half of the fairway will give a better view of the green and the pin, and the rough on the left is possibly less severe; but you must keep away from that right side. The first demand this hole makes is that you get in one of your very best drives, in the middle of the fairway, and so leave yourself with a feasible second shot. The third on the Ailsa is indeed one of the most perfect 'natural' holes in golf, forcefully illustrating how the terrain can be just as hazardous as anything man-made.

From about 80 yards up to the green, the ground is very broken, with quite pronounced mounds to the right. There is a greenside bunker, left centre, which cannot be seen from the left side of the fairway. There are two rather sticky bunkers at

the right front which also cannot be seen too clearly, so we are talking of a rather narrow target entrance. The average player may well land the ball short, hoping to tumble it on to the putting surface. A better player might hope to fly the ball to the middle of the green for a safe par, but the less-than-good player will frankly have problems.

In a championship, a prime pin position would be tight on the right side, making it very difficult for anyone who has

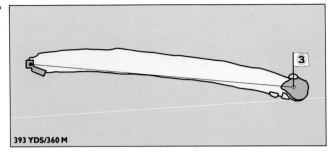

393 YDS/360 M

Keep left to open up the green

Ground falls away on the right into severe rough

2nd shot at the 3rd

Spectacular scenery behind the fairway

driven on the right side of the fairway, with those two right-hand bunkers closing out the second shot. The latter would have to be a high, soft fade to keep the ball in control and get somewhere close to the flag, and we had better assume that not too many people have that shot in the bag. So, if you get Blaw Wearie behind you with not more than a five on the card, you may sigh with some relief and be well pleased with yourself.

What's in the name?

Blaw Wearie means 'out of breath', which will be your fate on a windy day, for the wind here usually blows dead against.

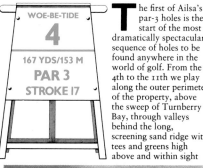

WOE-BE-TIDE

4

167 YDS/153 M

PAR 3

STROKE 17

The first of Ailsa's par-3 holes is the start of the most dramatically spectacular sequence of holes to be found anywhere in the world of golf. From the 4th to the 11th we play along the outer perimeter of the property, above the sweep of Turnberry Bay, through valleys behind the long, screening sand ridge with tees and greens high above and within sight of the ocean, to the rocky cliffs and coves of 'Bruce's Castle' and the Turnberry lighthouse, and beyond.

The fourth tee is at water level, hard by the beach, and the line to the green is along the shore, across the edge of a little bay. A pulpit green is cut into the left (seaward) side of a huge mound with a steep, tangled slope falling away to the shore on the left. On the face of the mound, apparently covering the right half of the green, is a vast bunker. We might call this a heroic hole, in the sense that there is nowhere you can miss the green without penalty. Success can only be bought with courage. To make a par or better, you must hit and hold the green with the tee shot, and you should find the green on

Small figures on the green emphasize the depth of the bunker

Steep, tangled slope to snare anything wandering to the left

from the 4th tee

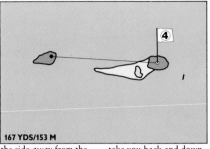

167 YDS/153 M

the side *away* from the pin. If the pin is cut on the left side of the green, shoot for the right side. If the pin is on the right, aim for the centre or left half of the green.

If you miss on the left with the pin on the left, you will go down a horrible bank. From there it will be a major achievement to get on in two, let alone arrive anywhere close to the flagstick. If you miss on the right, and find yourself tangled up on the mound, it will be quite difficult to get your second close to the pin. And if you carry that big bunker and are short of the green, the slope of the ground may well take you back and down into the bunker.

Over the back of the green is a slight downslope, perhaps not severe enough to be considered any kind of a hazard, and the essential requirement here is to be straight and go for the middle back of the green. The hole is totally exposed to the weather, so give some thought to that, also to pin position and to your yardage. Above all remember: there is no alternative to being on if you want the par. The hole does make one meagre gesture towards the player. The green is slightly saucered, and will tend to gather the ball into the centre.

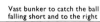

What's in the name?

Woe-be-tide tells you playfully to watch out, or the lurking waters of the Firth could be your downfall.

High mound protecting the right side of the green

Vast bunker to catch the ball falling short and to the right

FIN ME OOT

5

411 YDS/376 M

PAR 4

STROKE 3

By contrast with the previous hole, the fifth runs along a lovely valley, sheltered on the left by that high sand ridge above Turnberry beach which runs a good mile or more all the way to the eighth. The fifth was originally a par 5, but for the Open Championship of 1977 the back tee was abandoned, a tee just over the mound from the fourth green was used, and the hole was reduced by some 70–80 yards to become a par 4. As a par 5 it required two straightforward shots up the fairway,

then a half-left turn and a pitch to an ample green. As a par 4, I think it is a rather better hole, with most of the emphasis on the second shot.

All along the left side of this hole, rising up the sand ridge, is heavy rough. The whole thrust of design of the present hole will influence you to play down the right side all the way. And if there is wind from the sea, that will help force you right. I have to confess, however, that in the last round of the 1979 European Open I drove into the left rough,

advanced my second shot towards the green but still in the rough, and from there took a sand wedge and knocked the ball straight out, on to the green, and into the hole for a birdie! A birdie is a birdie at any time, but this is not the recommended route for the fifth hole.

Your driving line should be on the hut, up on the ridge by the 18th tee. There are two bunkers on the left side of the fairway, one at about 165 yards which is irrelevant and should not trouble you, another at around 215 yards which might. Keep to the right

of this bunker – there is ample fairway space. From that bunker, you are looking at a shot of some 170 yards to the centre of the green. The angle of approach for that shot is across the green (whereas the angle of the third shot when the hole was a par 5 was along the length of the green), and the front left has been closed off by two awkward little pot bunkers, nudging the putting surface, which must be carried.

There is a bunker at right front, rather wide, about 10 yards from the putting surface. Between that bunker and the two

Awkward pot-bunkers closing the front left

Approach to the 5th Green

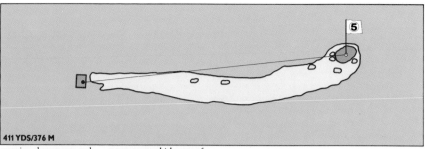

411 YDS/376 M

pots is a decent gap and it may be good tactics, if you are scared of making the carry, to target that space, then chip from there to the flag.

There is a substantial bunker 50 yards out, to the left, but I would think no longer really in play and another at the back right of the green, which is generously large. It slopes up from the front, levels off across the back half, and slopes down from the right through a flat central belly, then slightly up again on the left side. There is ample clear space through the green, which nestles in a huge arena or amphitheatre of sand dunes.

What's in the name?

The 5th hole does not easily disclose its secrets, so: 'Find me out.'

Target area for those worried about carrying the bunkers

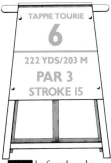

TAPPIE TOURIE
6
222 YDS/203 M
PAR 3
STROKE 15

The first thought you should have when you look at this hole, and the wisest decision you may make in the entire round, is to dub it a par 4 and play it accordingly. In harshness and severity it must rank with the 16th at Carnoustie. There is nowhere to go but the green, but you may find getting there very, very demanding.

The defences of the hole are threefold. First is the distance. A variety of tees can make it play anything from 190 yards to 250. You are playing across a valley to a green set into the sand ridge, and appreciably above you. Second are the fortifications – the bunkering, the slopes, the contours of the green and its surroundings. Third is the wind. If it is dead against, you must use a driver from the tee if you persist in thinking this can be a par 3; if from left to right, which is more or less prevailing, your shot will be drifted or thrown to the right, which is stiff with hazards, natural and man-made. So, by any judgment, you are facing a king-sized hole.

There is a very large bunker, set in the rough just left of a direct line, at 185 yards. Into a headwind it might well be in play. Short right of the green, on an upslope, there is a cavernous trap. Pitch in there, and you are likely to be plugged and have a fearsome task

to get out. The slope up to the green will gather any short shot towards that trap, and it will be a very difficult shot to advance the ball and to get it out and up to the green very much above the bunker. A little grassy swale to the left of the green was formerly a safety area, but that was sealed off by two tight, deep pot bunkers, put there for the Open Championship of 1977. So if you still insist that this is a par 3, there is virtually nowhere to go on Tappie Tourie but the putting surface.

The green is a decent size, sloping sharply up from the front to the centre, then only slightly up to the back. It slopes in to the centre from the left side, and if you were to carry the tee shot over and beyond the bunker, you could pitch slightly off the green, and see the ball break left, and on.

Pot-bunkers close the left side

From the 6th Tee

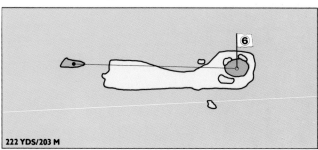

222 YDS/203 M

I must say, however, that if the weather conditions are against you or you have the slightest doubt about making the carry to the green, the sensible thing is to hit an iron shot to the bottom of the slope in front of the green, pitch up, look for a single putt but be well content with two.

However you do it, if you make three you can jump for joy. It is a very harsh golf hole.

What's in the name?

A 'tourie' means a 'thing on top', such as a bobble on a cap, so the name probably calls for a 'hit to the top', ie the high green.

Playing from below that awesome bunker on the right

Cavernous bunker and steep slope protect the right

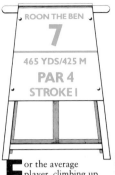

ROON THE BEN

7

465 YDS/425 M

PAR 4
STROKE I

For the average player, climbing up on this tee and surveying the prospect ahead, the first emotion could well be one of terror – and it would be entirely valid!

No matter what is said and written of the much-publicized and praised 9th and 10th tees, I suspect that this may be the most dramatic point in the course. High above the beach, the tee offers a stunning prospect, away to the left, of the wide Firth of Clyde, with islands and mountains and wheeling seabirds. But the hole itself surely dominates all. Falling away immediately in front of the tee is a tumbled broken valley with Wilson's Burn running through it. Beyond, the fairway starts and rises through a slight saddle in the dunes then dog-legs sharply to the left, continuing on up a long, rolling valley and climbing to a distant green. The initial carry over the valley is only some 150 yards, and to the saddle where the hole turns is perhaps little more than 200 yards. But it is the prospect that is disquieting.

So we should give it some sensible thought before we tackle it. Measured, I imagine very tightly, from the medal tee, it is listed at 465 yards, and you would do well, as at the previous hole, to make your own par – under almost any conditions call that five – and play the hole accordingly.

The first requirement is to drive up to and, if possible, over the saddle, the first decision whether or not you can carry or pass an evil bunker set in the left angle. It is 225 yards from the medal tee. There is space to the right of it, but if you should drive too far across the angle of the fairway, two bunkers on the far side, at 235 and 245 yards' range, will nail you. The rough inside the angle, and all along the left side, is very rough indeed. The left-hand bunker is penal, very large, very deep. If you are in that general area, you can call it a shot lost – all you can do is splash out of bunker or rough to the fairway, and still have 250 yards to go.

Position A from the tee might therefore be on or over the centre of the saddle, but not too far make that position with a 4-wood or a 3-iron, no matter where you find yourself here, the second shot will be a smash with the longest wood you have. In his final Open Championship round in 1977, having driven from the championship tee,

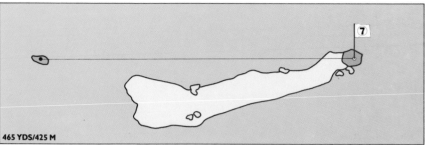

465 YDS/425 M

Tom Watson hit a driver from the fairway to make the green and a birdie, two astonishing blows.

This second shot demands some care and tactical thinking. About 150 yards on, some 100 yards from the green, is a bunker only just in the left rough, which perhaps should not be in play. There are two more by the green, slightly to the right and slightly short, amongst some mounds and slopes coming down from the right. The impression is of everything funnelling in towards the green. Beyond that bunker on the left is a very deep rough-strewn valley. Keep away. You could die down there and never be missed. If you are uncertain, make sure your shot goes right. You could be 50 yards wide to the right and still hit the green in three from light rough. The most sensible course for your second shot is aimed at the greenside bunkers, and short, whence you pitch on and make a relaxed five.

There is a good deal of movement in the back half of the green, with positive contouring. The front half is easier to putt, so pin position and some extra concentration on the green are important. Conservative positional play is the key to success on this hole. By all means make a birdie if you can, but do not seek to emulate Mr Watson on the second shot.

What's in the name?

'Round the mountain' is the intended drift here, not that you will need the attentions of a Strathclyde sanatorium.

Left:
Breathtaking view
of the fairway

Target area for the safety shot, but still a long way to go

Bunker and dangerous rough on the left

More bunkers on the right

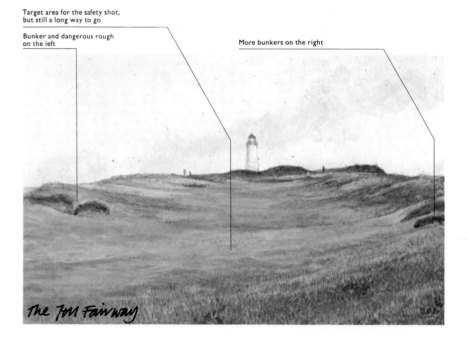

The JW Fairway

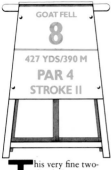

GOAT FELL
8
427 YDS/390 M
PAR 4
STROKE II

This very fine two-shot hole presents a drive completely dominated by one single fairway bunker. This is the last of the set of holes screened on the left by the long sand ridge above the beach, and the entire fairway slopes down from it, from the left, as though pointing everything towards that solitary bunker. It is beautifully placed, 250 yards out from the medal tee, and some 10–15 yards in from the edge of the rough.

For a professional or first-class amateur, particularly downwind, the plan would be to carry that bunker, or at least get past it, for the best possible sight of the green. Without being a dog-leg, the hole does turn slightly to the left. The average player will probably not reach the bunker, so his plan should be to drive along the left side, even marginally off the fairway, since the contouring, even from the light rough, will bring the ball back down into play.

The second shot can

Closer in to the green, showing the treacherous left-hand bunker

Bunker and general danger area

2nd Shot at the 8th

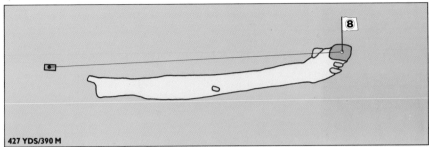

427 YDS/390 M

Dead ground makes distance deceptive

be deceptive. There is quite a large valley of 'dead' ground in front of the green which is set up high, and goes right back to the edge of a cliff. On the second shot, I would be inclined to take a club and a half, or even two clubs, more than you think at first glance, since you then have a chance to chase or scuffle the ball through the valley and up the slope to the green. Two large bunkers are set into the face of a big sand dune at the right front of the green, and there is one deep bunker 20 yards short on the left. The general area of that bunker is very dangerous – miss or be short if you must, but again favour the right side. The green is quite ample, with a slight ridge through it.

You will be asked for two big shots on this hole, quite possibly two woods, but it is an honest, open hole, asking only for honest, straightforward shot-making.

What's in the name?

Goat Fell takes its name from the tallest peak on the Island of Arran, across the Firth to the north-west.

BRUCE'S CASTLE

9

413 YDS/378 M

PAR 4
STROKE 7

The most photographed of all Turnberry's delights, and one of the most photographed tees in golf, the championship tee of the ninth hole on the Ailsa course, perched out on a rocky promontory of cliff with sheer drops of 50 feet or more to the shore below, is a paradox, and possibly a fraud. Mackenzie Ross, the architect of Ailsa,

designed the hole to be played from the medal tee, and this championship tee, behind and slightly below, came later. It is entirely spectacular and marvellously theatrical, but the visual effects may not have much bearing on how you play the hole.

By all means, if you do not suffer from vertigo, stand on it and enjoy the prospect, and if you feel particularly

resolute and indomitable at the time, by all means play from it. You will see very little of the fairway. You will be obliged to carry the best part of 200 yards, over an inlet of the sea, to a stone cairn marker set on the rise opposite. Put your faith in your Maker, the marker, and your swing, and go for it. If you are a long hitter, aim 10 yards left of the marker to get to the left side of the fairway, where the lighthouse will loom above you, and you will discover there an open shot to the green.

From the medal tee your carry will be some 150 yards to the marker, your line directly on it. You may see only the top of the flagstick from the tee, and the absolutely perfect line is on the war memorial behind the green.

There is a lot of movement in this fairway – some players believe too much – and it is not much more than 20 yards wide at its

The view from the medal tee

From the Championship Tee at the 9th

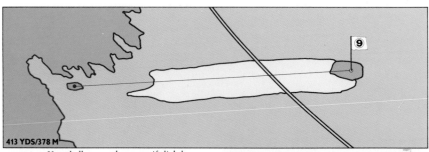

413 YDS/378 M

narrowest. Your ball can
be rather thrown about.
If you hook badly left of
line, you can be in
troublesome rough. Slice
to the right, and there is
even more trouble with
the ground falling away
From that side you will
be blocked off from the
green by some mounds
protecting it on the right
front – again Mackenzie
Ross has produced a
stiff, well-protected hole
without using one single
bunker.

The shot to the green,
then, should come in
from the left. From that
direction you have a
very reasonable target:

the green, if slightly
narrow, is the best part
of 45 yards long. The
real challenge of the hole
is the drive, and the
anguish you may feel on
the tee. You can
overstress this to
yourself. A positive,
correct, firm strike at the
ball from the tee, and
you have broken the
back of the hole.

What's in the name?

**Bruce is Robert the
Bruce, Scottish king
from 1306–29. Remains
of his castle lie between
the 8th green and the
9th tee.**

War memorial behind the
green

The undefended green

200 yards to the stone cairn

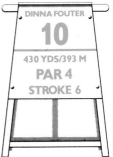

DINNA FOUTER

10

430 YDS/393 M

PAR 4
STROKE 6

The tenth tee is possibly even more theatrical than the ninth. Before you lie the now familiar seascapes to the west and north, the lighthouse, the familiar symbol of Turnberry just behind, the ripe, rolling hillsides of South Ayrshire ahead, while beneath you, rolling round a bay of rocks and sand, is the marvellous tenth hole. It sweeps round what looks like a great semi-circle, with every hazard in view.

In the driving area, there are no fairway bunkers, giving ample

The fairway, the bay and the Ayrshire hills

From the Fairway Bunker at the 10.

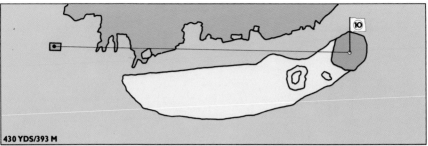

430 YDS/393 M

space to manoeuvre. All you need to decide is how closely you dare skirt the left side, and the beach, with your tee shot. As on so many other holes on the Ailsa, the architecture and the ground indicate that you should play to the right.

Dominating the hole visually, and certainly compromising the second shot, is a massive circular fairway bunker that fills almost the entire width of the fairway, with an 'island' of grass in the centre. Here more than anywhere is demonstrated a famous Ailsa signature – the 'bearded' or 'whiskered'

bunker, the long marram grass left growing round the fringes and giving that effect. This bunker is 25 yards from front to back. The back is 65 yards from the centre of the green, so you must seek to dismiss it completely by flying your second shot over it.

Since the best access to this green is from the right, another smaller bunker is set strategically beyond the big one, to defend that right side. But it is still 40 yards from the centre of the green, 20 yards from the front edge, so you have a margin there for your second shot.

Your biggest problem on this hole may well be this second shot, and the psychological block you may have in looking ahead to the bunkers and contemplating what you can do about them. Force yourself to ignore them and hit a full shot to the green. You could pitch as much as 20 yards short and run on. The green is very big. If you have driven anywhere on the left side of the fairway, you must shoot your second at the right half of the green. The green will be kind to you except on the left, where there is a rather quick slope down into

rough grass. So trend to the right, and let fly boldly at the green, even if you have a 4- or 5-wood. Don't worry about going past the flag. This is a hole where you must venture bravely if you are to succeed.

What's in the name?

'Don't mess about' is the firm instruction for this hole, particularly when going for the green.

Ground slopes away to the left

Bunker defending the right-side approach

MAIDENS

11

137 YDS/125 M

PAR 3

STROKE 18

This is the last of that incomparable run of seaward holes which started back at the fourth. Again, it is worth having a look at the championship tee, a pulpit perched on a rocky outcrop rather like the back tee at the ninth, with the same wonderful vistas surrounding you. To the south, you look across the vast fields of gorse encompassing the Arran course to the Turnberry Hotel, with its dazzling white walls and red tiles, stretched along the ridge that overlooks the entire property.

The medal tee is 137 yards, the championship tee 40 yards further back, and if I were you, I would play the hole from the latter. It makes it much more challenging, particularly if you find yourself hitting into wind. From the medal tee, the hole is obviously just a short pop.

'Maidens' is a delightful and very attractive short hole. The green is reasonable in size for a par 3, with a good deal of width. There is one long bunker which closes off most of the left half at the front, and two more covering the right, centre and back, but towards the right front of the green you have a good entrance, and on this hole you must certainly expect to make par, and have a fair shot at a birdie. The important thing to be sure of here is that you select the right club for the prevailing conditions.

The green is set just in front of a quarry, and many people believe it should be set further back, more into the quarry. I daresay that might make for greenkeeping problems, and I for one am content with things as they are. I see no reason to fiddle about with a very pretty and very friendly short hole.

Large bunker closing off the left side of the green

The 11th Green

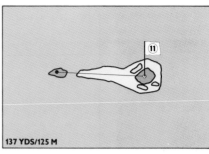

137 YDS/125 M

A panoramic view from
the tee

What's in the name?

Local geography is the
key: Maidens is the
village to the north of
the course.

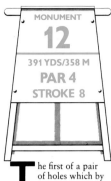

MONUMENT

12

391 YDS/358 M

PAR 4

STROKE 8

The first of a pair of holes which by Turnberry standards are flat, and form a respite from the preceding three or four holes and a breather before the big finish to come, the 12th is a straight par 4 down a fairly narrow fairway. I find it a rather oddly designed hole, and have the feeling that it has not quite kept pace with the

modern game and the first-class player, as has the Ailsa course in general. That may not worry the average player overmuch.

There is a pair of bunkers on the left side of the fairway at 175–180 yards which normally should not be in play. Beyond them on the same side is a good-sized bunker at 250 yards which will be out of range for most Turnberry players and in certain conditions would be difficult even for professionals to reach. The right side of the fairway is completely unprotected. This you must use to your advantage by making the right half your destination from the tee. The driving line should be to the right of that first pair of bunkers, and perhaps slightly left of

the monument on the hill above and to the right of the green.

Along that right side is a good 10 yards of light rough, and even at the height of summer growth, it should allow

The defences around the green

you a decent shot out of it. In fact if the 12th tee were placed up on the plateau above the 11th green, as some have

Watch for subtle borrows on this green

2nd shot at the 12th

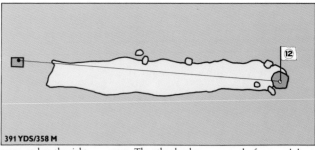

391 YDS/358 M

suggested, it would add only some 25 yards to the hole, maintain it as a par 4 and make the drive into a more pronounced dog-leg to the left. If this were done, the present bunkering might have to move, and on the right new bunkers, or better still a stretch of gorse bushes, would have to be considered, at around 220–250 yards. This I think would make it a much more dramatic hole.

The present approach to the green, from that right side, is defended inevitably by a bunker 30 yards short, and a secondary bunker close by the right front of the green. The other bunker you see 30 yards short on the left is so wide as to be of no great consequence. From a point level with the second left-side fairway bunker, you will be exactly 200 yards from the centre of the green, so even with your best drive, you will be looking for a healthy hit with your second.

The green is built up, with a dip then a slope up to the front, and the important thing is to have enough club to get you there. Be quite sure of your yardage and your club selection, and try to be past the pin – behind the green is a slight rise which should stop the long shot. The green slopes slightly left to right, and extra care is needed when putting. This green does have some quite subtle borrows.

What's in the name?

The Monument on the hill above the green commemorates the airmen of two world wars stationed at Turnberry.

Target area for the drive to the right of the fairway

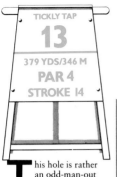

TICKLY TAP
13
379 YDS/346 M
PAR 4
STROKE 14

This hole is rather an odd-man-out on the Ailsa in that it is quite flat, and is a drive and a short pitch, one of the shortest par-4 holes on the course. It is dominated by a grassy hollow and a ridge on the right, which contains a lusty bunker, some 225 yards out, at the angle of the right dog-leg. There is ample fairway space to the left here, as much as 50 yards in places as it swings round to the right, and beyond the angle, about 280 yards out, is another substantial bunker, this

Target area for the drive
inside the left-hand bunker

No bunkers around the green
but a difficult surface to hold

2nd shot at the 13th

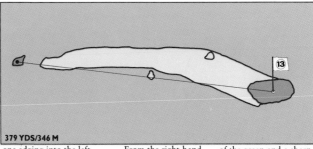

379 YDS/346 M

The green has some
subtle borrows

Ridge and bunker at 225 yards

one edging into the left
fairway.

You must obviously
play to the left of that
right-side bunker, and
your aiming point might
well be the more distant
trap, on the left. But
what must concern you
most on this tee are the
ground conditions – wet
or dry, slow or fast – and
the overhead conditions,
particularly the wind. If
you play the hole in
summer, with hard
ground and down a stiff
breeze from the north-
west, your ball may skip
all the way to that left
bunker. At any time of
the year, you must avoid
the rough on the right.

From the right-hand
bunker to the centre of
the green is 145 yards.
From the left-hand
bunker to the centre of
the green is 100 yards, so
some kind of pitch shot
is on. The green is free of
all bunkering. It is in fact
a plateau, raised some
three feet above what
looks like a plain level
fairway. You can see all
of the green save the far
left-hand corner, and the
whole thing is flat,
possibly just sloping
away from you
fractionally. However,
the defences are there,
even if they are subtle
and not obvious. There
is a slight dip in front

of the green and a sharp
rise up to the putting
surface. And the green is
set diagonally across the
shot, from 4 o'clock to
10 o'clock. All of this,
particularly downwind,
with nothing much at the
back to check the ball,
makes this approach shot
testing, and perhaps
rather difficult to stop.
You might even consider
under-clubbing slightly.

What's in the name?

A subtle hole, most of all
at the approach to the
green where you will be
faced with a 'tricky little
hit'.

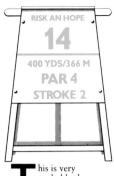

RISK AN HOPE

14

400 YDS/366 M

PAR 4

STROKE 2

This is very probably the most extreme par 4 on the course, and you would do well to 'hope' rather more than you 'risk'. Into any kind of wind at all, it will demand two very fine hits, even from a professional, so before you pull anything out of the bag on this tee, accept that you are about to play a par 5 hole, or, at best, a par 4.5.

In the short driving zone, the fairway is very narrow. In the long driving zone, the fairway is also very narrow. In between there is a reasonable sector of friendly space. Dominating the drive, 150 yards from the tee, is a bunker on the left and a solid mass of gorse on the right. The gap between is little more than 15 yards, and you must get through there, or over it. Beyond that gap the fairway spreads itself nicely, but from about 220 yards on, it shrinks again to about 20 yards across. Through the original gap, especially towards the right half, there is a flat area and that is where you must be. The rough on the right side of this hole can be quite punishing.

The green – it looks miles away – is strongly defended centre-right and centre-left by particularly strong, deep bunkers. An exceptionally big fairway trap covers the centre-left of the green. It is a good 10 yards deep from front to back, and leaves only some 10 yards from its back point to the edge of the putting surface. Into wind, you will be well advised to – and may have to – play short of it with your second, then pitch over it. Even in still air you will want a very fine second shot to carry it. And if you have persuaded yourself that you are really playing a par 5, I suggest you hit your second shot on the

The 14th – Risk an' Hope

line of the right-hand bunker, to be just short of it. Then you will have an open third into the green, and may make it with one putt for a 'birdie'.

The green is large and wide and slopes towards you, so if your shot to the green is to be your third, then you have plenty of room in which to work and get it fairly close to the pin.

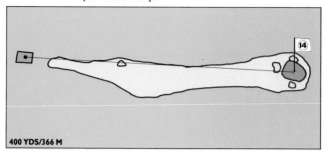

400 YDS/366 M

What's in the name?

This hole is true to its daunting label, for your first two hits must be both bold and very good.

Deep bunkers protect the green on both the left and right sides

2nd shot at the 14th

Narrow fairway

Punishing rough on the right

Left:
A view from the tee showing the bunker
at 150 yards

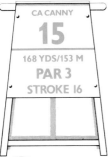

CA CANNY

15

168 YDS/153 M
PAR 3
STROKE 16

Ca' Canny is the perfect example of a very demanding, and punishing, short hole. As the professionals say, there is 'nowhere to miss', nowhere but the green to be if you are to avoid serious trouble.

From the medal tee it plays at 168 yards – from the championship tee more than 200 – and into a strong headwind you may well need anything up to and including a driver. Wind and weather conditions again can be decisive here. The green is set into a sand dune which overlooks it slightly at the left side and the back, but in practical terms the green is unsheltered. There is a very sharp and steep slope to the right, plunging down towards the 8th fairway in a good 30-foot drop. There is no usable ground between tee and green, unless you care for an ocean of heather, and the hole demands a shot carried all the way to the putting surface. Finally, there are three very deep bunkers all along the left side, and the last of the 'Ca' Canny' ramparts is another deep trap, positioned front-right at the top of the downslope, and put in specifically for the 1977

The 15th Green

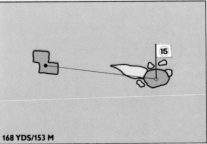

168 YDS/153 M

The two deep bunkers
at the front of the green

The middle of the green is the
only place to go

Open Championship.
It immediately
became a controversial
bunker. Many contended
that in a championship a
loose shot could be held
by it, whereas if it wasn't
there the ball would kick
far down the slope into
rough ground. They
suggested that such is the
skill of the modern
professional playing from
sand that a bunker shot
would be that much
easier for him than
trying to recover from
rough 30 feet below the
putting surface. They
were probably right. The
severity of this slope will
certainly take the ball all
the way to the bottom,
and that usually means

an instant four.
The green is 35 yards
from front to back and
reasonably wide. It helps
you a little from the left
side, taking the ball into
the centre, and also
slopes up towards the
back, which will help
hold the shot. But you
will get little else in the
way of help from this
hole, and the main
object is simply to hit
confidently for the
middle of the green – and
get there.

What's in the name?
'Take care' is the
watchword. Any error at
the 15th comes in for
heavy punishment.

Apleasant little hole for the professionals, who would consider it no more than a 'drive and a flick' in normal circumstances, but a fearful hole for the average player. In fact fear, the fear that Wilson's Burn puts into the mind of the player, is the real and only defence of this hole.

There is one bunker set into the left side of the fairway, just over 200 yards out. Then there is the burn. No one now seems to know who Wilson was, but his burn runs along the bottom of a ravine which crosses the front of the green. The burn itself is not particularly deep, but the ravine is, with rather steep sides. It has the same effect as the rather more famous Swilcan Burn at the first hole of the Old Course – it is there, and it has to be crossed. Anything over-short can dribble down the near bank and into the water. Anything that carries the burn but is not positively 'up' on the green, will dribble back down the far bank, and into the water. Although it is a substantial physical barrier, the problem for the player is

Aim for the centre-back of the green

The 16th Green and Wilson's Burn

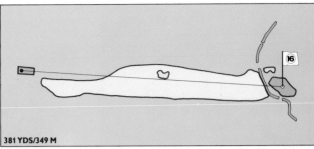

381 YDS/349 M

The ravine in front of the green is a daunting prospect

best driving line would be on the dome-shaped shelter you see beyond the 17th tee. The rough on the left can be quite strong. Keep away from this side. You can miss by miles on the right, and still have a shot at the green, even if you go all the way wide to the 7th fairway.

There are sand hills to the left of, and behind, the green, which is quite large and a good 35 yards from front to back. On this hole, you can see everything before you,

psychological – created by the prospect and the possibilities in the terrain rather than by the terrain itself.

The bunker on the left is reachable, so keep right from the tee. The

see the green from the tee. The key is the second shot. If the flagstick is cut near the front, close to the downslope into the burn, don't be too clever – hit a full shot with whatever club you decide is needed to get to the back-centre of the green and rely on a two-putt par. If you are downwind, that is, with a northerly wind, you might have a straightforward short pitch to this green. If you are into wind (a southerly), you might well need a second wood. And if you are not

entirely certain, for any reason, that you can make the carry, do not force it. Lay up short of the burn in two, and think of a little pitch over – and why not think positively then of a single putt? But if you do not make par here do not grieve – it is not all that easy, and the next hole should console you.

What's in the name?
The 'little burn' or stream is Wilson's Burn – not so wee when you have to carry it or suffer the consequences.

Approach shot must carry this bank or the ball will run back into the burn

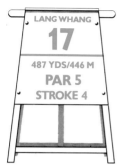

LANG WHANG
17
487 YDS/446 M
PAR 5
STROKE 4

L ang Whang is yet another Ailsa hole which essentially uses the terrain and its natural contours more than man-made hazards. The second par 5 on the course, the only one on this inward half, it can look a good deal more intimidating than it really is.

A high sand ridge runs along most of the left side. To the right, another broken mass of sand dunes reaches over towards the sixth green. These sand hills almost but not quite join in front of the 17th tee, leaving a gap and a path

along which we reach the fairway proper. The view from the tee, across the bridge from the 16th green, lets us see only a slice of the left half of the fairway. Immediately in front of the tee, falling beneath us, Wilson's Burn in its deep valley winds away across the 7th fairway to the sea. Since the 17th tee seems high above all this, you may feel unprotected and friendless as you stand there and look towards the green. But don't be downcast – the gap ahead of you is a carry of only 100 yards and beyond it is a valley of

fairway as wide as you could wish.

In this great expanse of fairway is one bunker, to the right, at 265 yards. It is so far and so wide that you can forget it. The next fairway bunker you see, ahead of you, is the key point of the entire hole. At 375 yards, a high, strong ridge comes in from the right, narrowing down the fairway to a tight 20 yards or so. The bunker is set in the end face of this ridge, squeezing the fairway into an uphill gap; it then becomes narrow, level or slightly uphill, all the way to the

The bunker in the end of the ridge and the narrow uphill fairway

green. If you get off a good drive, say 225 yards, you will then be 150 yards from that bunker, which in turn is 100 yards from the green.

The bunker in question might, incidentally, make a good driving line. There are no hazards behind it, save an uneven, rolling, rather up-and-down stretch of fairway. Before you get into your second shot would be a good moment to stop and think what you are

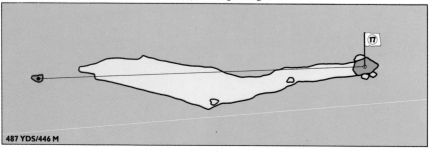

487 YDS/446 M

The 17th Fairway

Fairway narrows to 20 yards

Bunker set in the face of the high ridge

about. The next critical factor is the green, strongly protected by one big trap on the left, and two on the right, but with a very open front. It is of medium width, but quite long – 35 yards. So you have a fair chance of hitting and holding it with a third shot.

The 17th is, I feel, an attractive hole for the average player who should be confident of making par if he is thinking rationally. But the real examination is on the second shot – how that key bunker and its narrow, uphill gap are played. The prevailing wind will be against you, and into wind you might think it sensible to be just short of it, reaching the bottom of the slope in two, then making a longish pitch to the green from there. Downwind, you may well decide that you can ignore it and fly the ball well past it. Such are the fascinating dilemmas posed here by terrain and weather.

What's in the name?

A 'good whack' is called for here, to set yourself a reasonable chance of making the green in three.

AILSA HAME

18

377 YDS/345 M

PAR 4

STROKE 12

Almost there. Almost finished with the Ailsa – but not quite. The red tops and white walls of the Dormy House and the Turnberry Hotel may give you thoughts of other pleasures, but there is still a furlong or two to go.

Stand on the medal tee of the 18th and you may feel the last pangs of Ailsa terror, such as you felt at the 7th or the 9th, for you are on top of the sweeping ridge which forms an amphitheatre around the 5th green, beneath you to the right. And you are facing a tee shot across a sector of that ridge, presenting in front of

you what looks like a wall of heather and rough, with a path to the Dormy House running along the top.

Fortunately, the carry over that lot is no more than 100 yards and you are playing a hole which is honest and open, a perfectly pleasant finishing hole with

everything in view before you. For the Open Championship and major professional tournaments, the 18th tee of the Arran course,

Uneven fairway but no other greenside hazards

Deep rough on the right

The 18th Green and the Turnberry Hotel

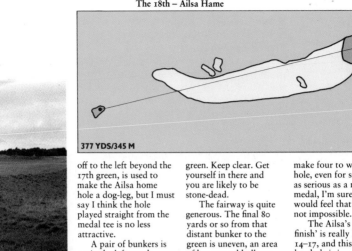

377 YDS/345 M

Putting out – a view from the left back of the green

off to the left beyond the 17th green, is used to make the Ailsa home hole a dog-leg, but I must say I think the hole played straight from the medal tee is no less attractive.

A pair of bunkers is set in the left rough covering the range 165–185 yards and I would expect you to pass them to the right. A distant bunker on the right, should not be in play, but it makes a good driving line from the medal tee. Perhaps the greatest danger on this hole is a very heavy bank of gorse along the right side, quite close to the fairway and running from about 175 yards almost all the way to the green. Keep clear. Get yourself in there and you are likely to be stone-dead.

The fairway is quite generous. The final 80 yards or so from that distant bunker to the green is uneven, an area of humps and hollows, but there are no greenside sand hazards. There are some swales around most of the green which might make short chip shots slightly tricky if you miss the green, but even from one of your less-than-perfect drives, you might reasonably be thinking of reaching this green, and making the par. It is in truth an inviting green to hit to, and if you were required to

make four to win on this hole, even for something as serious as a monthly medal, I'm sure you would feel that it was not impossible.

The Ailsa's 'big finish' is really holes 14–17, and this gentle last hole is just the kind of thing to send you off thinking that, on one of the world's finest golf courses, perhaps you didn't do too badly after all.

What's in the name?
The home hole on the Ailsa course – open and straightforward just so long as you don't rush it.

The Ailsa Course of the Turnberry Hotel must now be considered with Royal Troon as the classic West of Scotland Open Championship venue. Although it had staged professional events, including the Match Play Championship, and an Amateur Championship and Walker Cup matches, it was not until 1977 that it became an 'Open' course. In the event, it produced one of the most dramatic of all Open Championships – Tom Watson and Jack Nicklaus battled each other with brilliant stroke-making until Watson prevailed by only one stroke with a record aggregate score.

1
DUNLOP
DDH

Course Record (Ailsa Course)
63 Mark Hayes (USA)
(Open Championship 1977)

Open Championship
1977 Tom Watson (USA) 268

Double Diamond World of Golf Classic
1975 The Americas

European Open
1979 Sandy Lyle 275

PGA Club Professionals' Championship
1980 David Jagger 286

PGA Match Play Championship
1957 Christy O'Connor (Ireland)   1960 Eric Brown
1963 David Thomas

John Player Classic
1972 Bob Charles (New Zealand) 285   1973 Charles Coody (USA) 289

Amateur Championship
1961 M F Bonallack

Walker Cup
1963 GB 8   USA 12
(Four matches halved)

Home Internationals
1960 England

Ladies' Amateur Championship
1912 Miss G Ravenscroft   1921 Miss C Leitch   1937 Miss J Anderson

Left: Miss Cecil Leitch, four times winner of the Ladies' Amateur Championship and winner at Turnberry in 1921

Top left: Michael Bonallack, winner of the 1961 Amateur
Championship at Turnberry, with his wife Angela who was the
beaten finalist in the Ladies' Amateur Championship at Royal
Birkdale the following year. Right: Deane Beman (USA) chipping
to the 16th green during the 1963 Walker Cup match.
Above: David Thomas, 1963 PGA Match Play Champion

Above and right: Gale force winds tore up the tented village
at the 1973 John Player Classic but order was restored and
Charles Coody took the trophy

Top: The 5th green during the 1977 Open. Above: Tom Watson and Jack Nicklaus who played almost stroke for stroke through all four rounds. Left: Tom Watson the 1977 Open Champion. Right: Sandy Lyle, winner of the 1979 European Open, is presented with the trophy by 1978 winner Bobby Wadkins

Playing the course Guests of the Turnberry Hotel have preferential rates and exclusive access to the tee at certain times, but otherwise the course, like its partner the Arran, is open to everyone. These courses can be very busy in season, and advance reservations are recommended. These can be booked directly through Golf Course Reservation at Turnberry Hotel, Maidens Road, Turnberry, Girvan, Strathclyde KA26 9LT, tel Turnberry (06553) 202, or through the professional's shop at Turnberry, tel Turnberry (06553) 370. There are no restrictions on ladies' play.

Adjoining course The Arran, laid out 'inside' the bigger Ailsa course, is rather less dramatic, without the seascapes and tumbling dunes of the Ailsa, but providing a tight test between avenues of gorse.

Arran 6276 yards   SSS 70.

Recommended courses in the surrounding area The local course at Girvan (5 miles) is open and sporty, if short, and the Troon-Prestwick courses are within comfortable reach – Royal Troon, Prestwick, Western Gailes, Glasgow Gailes and the Kilmarnock GC at Barassie are particularly recommended.

Girvan GC, Municipal Golf Course Road, Girvan, Strathclyde; tel Girvan (0465) 4272.

Royal Troon GC, Troon, Strathclyde; tel Troon (0292) 311555.

Prestwick GC, Links Road, Prestwick, Strathclyde; tel Prestwick (0292) 77404.

Western Gailes GC, Gailes, Strathclyde; tel Irvine (0294) 311357.

Glasgow Gailes GC, Gailes, Strathclyde; tel Irvine (0294) 311347.

Kilmarnock GC (Barassie), Barassie, Troon, Strathclyde; tel Troon (0292) 311077.

Where to stay Turnberry Hotel can provide all of man's wants and needs, and there is more inexpensive accommodation at the Dormy House. The Caledonian Hotel in Ayr would be a good central point for all courses in this region.

Turnberry Hotel, Maidens Road, Turnberry, Girvan, Strathclyde KA26 9LT; tel Turnberry (06553) 202.

King's Arms, Dalrymple Street, Girvan, Strathclyde; tel Girvan (0465) 3322.

Caledonian Hotel, Ayr, Strathclyde; tel Ayr (0292) 69331, telex 76357.

Savoy Park Hotel, Ayr, Strathclyde; tel Ayr (0292) 66112/63469.

Turnberry